D1515400

Velociraptor

Kimberley Jane Pryor

Marshall Cavendish
Benchmark
New York

This edition first published in 2012 in the United States of America by Marshall Cavendish Benchmark
An imprint of Marshall Cavendish Corporation

Website: www.marshallcavendish.us

This publication represents the opinions and views of the author based on Kimberley Jane Pryor's personal experience, knowledge, and research. The information in this book serves as a general guide only. The author and publisher have used their best efforts in preparing this book and disclaim liability rising directly and indirectly from the use and application of this book.

Other Marshall Cavendish Offices:
Marshall Cavendish International (Asia) Private Limited, 1 New Industrial Road, Singapore 536196 • Marshall Cavendish International (Thailand) Co Ltd. 253 Asoke, 12th Flr, Sukhumvit 21 Road, Klongtoey Nua, Wattana, Bangkok 10110, Thailand • Marshall Cavendish (Malaysia) Sdn Bhd, Times Subang, Lot 46, Subang Hi-Tech Industrial Park, Batu Tiga, 40000 Shah Alam, Selangor Darul Ehsan, Malaysia

Marshall Cavendish is a trademark of Times Publishing Limited

Library of Congress Cataloging-in-Publication Data

Pryor, Kimberley Jane.
  Velociraptor / Kimberley Jane Pryor.
    p. cm. — (Discovering Dinosaurs)
  Summary: "Discusses the physical characteristics, time period, diet, and habitat of the Velociraptor" —Provided by publisher.
  Includes index.
  ISBN 978-1-60870-540-5
  1. Velociraptor—Juvenile literature. I. Title.
  QE862.S3P795 2012
  567.912—dc22
                                    2010037190

First published in 2011 by
MACMILLAN EDUCATION AUSTRALIA PTY LTD
15–19 Claremont Street, South Yarra 3141

Visit our website at www.macmillan.com.au or go directly to www.macmillanlibrary.com.au

Associated companies and representatives throughout the world.

Publisher: Carmel Heron
Commissioning Editor: Niki Horin
Managing Editor: Vanessa Lanaway
Editor: Laura Jeanne Gobal
Proofreader: Helena Newton
Designer: Kerri Wilson (cover and text)
Page Layout: Pier Vido and Domenic Lauricella
Photo Researcher: Brendan Gallagher
Illustrator: Melissa Webb
Production Controller: Vanessa Johnson

Printed in China

Acknowledgments
The author and publisher are grateful to the following for permission to reproduce copyright material:

Photographs courtesy of: Corbis/Walter Geiersperger, **8**; Getty Images/Louie Psihoyos, **29**; iStockphoto/Joe McDaniel, **9**; Photolibrary/Barbara Strnadova, **14**.

Background image of ripples on water © Shutterstock/ArchMan.

While every care has been taken to trace and acknowledge copyright, the publisher tenders their apologies for any accidental infringement where copyright has proved untraceable. They would be pleased to come to a suitable arrangement with the rightful owner in each case.

For Nick, Thomas, and Ashley

1 3 5 6 4 2

Contents

When a word is printed in **bold**, you can look up its meaning in the glossary on page 31.

What Are Dinosaurs?

Dinosaurs (*dy-no-soars*) were **reptiles** that lived millions of years ago. They were different from other reptiles because their legs were directly under their bodies instead of to their sides like today's reptiles. Dinosaurs walked or ran on land.

At one time, there were more than 1,000 different kinds of dinosaurs

Dinosaurs lived during a period of time called the Mesozoic (*mes-ah-zoh-ik*) Era. The Mesozoic Era is divided into the Triassic (*try-ass-ik*), Jurassic (*je-rass-ik*), and Cretaceous (*krah-tay-shahs*) periods.

This timeline shows the three different periods of the Mesozoic Era, when dinosaurs lived.

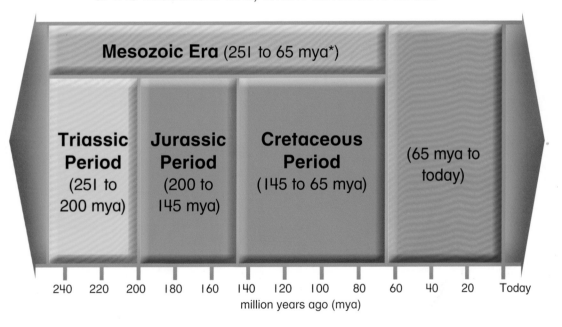

Mesozoic Era (251 to 65 mya*)

Triassic Period (251 to 200 mya)

Jurassic Period (200 to 145 mya)

Cretaceous Period (145 to 65 mya)

(65 mya to today)

240　220　200　180　160　140　120　100　80　60　40　20　Today

million years ago (mya)

*Note: mya = million years ago

Dinosaur Groups

Dinosaurs are sorted into two main groups according to their hipbones. Some dinosaurs had hipbones like a lizard's. Other dinosaurs had hipbones like a bird's.

All dinosaurs were either lizard-hipped or bird-hipped.

Dinosaurs

Lizard-hipped dinosaurs

Bird-hipped dinosaurs

Dinosaurs can be sorted into five smaller groups. Some lizard-hipped dinosaurs walked on two legs and ate meat. Others walked on four legs and ate plants. All bird-hipped dinosaurs ate plants.

Main Group	Smaller Group	Features	Examples
Lizard-hipped	Theropoda (*ther-ah-poh-dah*)	• Small to large • Walked on two legs • Meat-eaters	Tyrannosaurus Velociraptor
	Sauropodomorpha (*soar-rop-ah-dah-mor-fah*)	• Huge • Walked on four legs • Plant-eaters	Diplodocus
Bird-hipped	Thyreophora (*theer-ee-off-or-ah*)	• Small to large • Walked on four legs • Plant-eaters	Ankylosaurus
	Ornithopoda (*or-ni-thop-oh-dah*)	• Small to large • Walked on two or four legs • Plant-eaters	Muttaburrasaurus
	Ceratopsia (*ser-ah-top-see-ah*)	• Small to large • Walked on two or four legs • Plant-eaters • Frilled and horned skulls	Protoceratops

This table shows how dinosaurs can be sorted according to their size, how they walked and the food they ate.

How Do We Know about Dinosaurs?

We know about dinosaurs because people have found fossils. Fossils are the preserved remains of plants and animals that lived long ago. They include bones, teeth, footprints, and eggs.

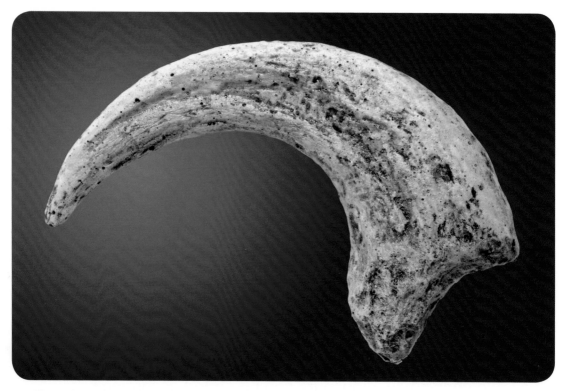

This fossil is the claw of a Velociraptor.

People who study fossils are called paleontologists (*pail-ee-on-tol-oh-jists*). They study fossils to learn about dinosaurs. They also remove dinosaur bones from rocks and rebuild **skeletons**.

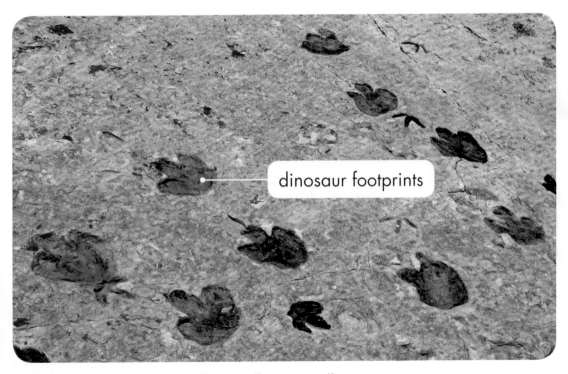

dinosaur footprints

Paleontologists sometimes discover dinosaur footprints, which are fossils, too.

Meet Velociraptor

Velociraptor (*ve-loss-uh-rap-tor*) was a small, lizard-hipped dinosaur. It belonged to a group of dinosaurs called theropoda. Dinosaurs in this group walked on two legs and ate meat.

Velociraptor was a small, fierce dinosaur.

Velociraptor lived in the late Cretaceous period, between 84 and 65 million years ago.

The purple area on this timeline shows when Velociraptor lived.

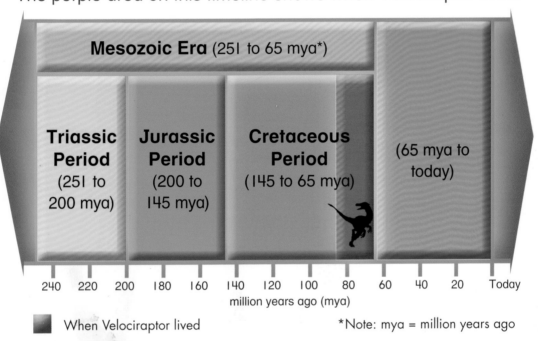

Mesozoic Era (251 to 65 mya*)

Triassic Period (251 to 200 mya)

Jurassic Period (200 to 145 mya)

Cretaceous Period (145 to 65 mya)

(65 mya to today)

240   220   200   180   160   140   120   100   80   60   40   20   Today

million years ago (mya)

When Velociraptor lived

*Note: mya = million years ago

What Did Velociraptor Look Like?

Velociraptor was 6 feet (1.8 meters) long and 1.6 feet (50 centimeters) tall at the hips. It weighed up to 33 pounds (15 kilograms).

Velociraptor was about the size and weight of an average dog.

Velociraptor walked on two legs. It had a long head and a long, stiff tail. Velociraptor had long, curved claws. It had feathers but could not fly.

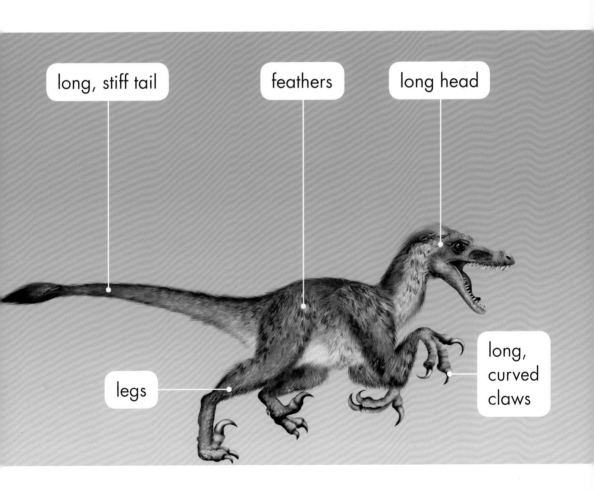

long, stiff tail

feathers

long head

legs

long, curved claws

The Skull and Senses of Velociraptor

Velociraptor had a very large skull and brain for its size. This meant that it was one of the smartest dinosaurs! Velociraptor had jaws lined with sharp, jagged teeth.

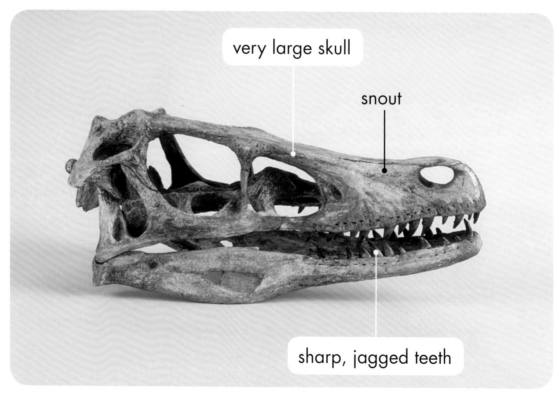

very large skull

snout

sharp, jagged teeth

Velociraptor had a long, flat snout.

Velociraptor had eyes in the front of its head. It used its eyes to judge the distance to its **prey**. Velociraptor also had very good **senses** of hearing and smell.

The Senses of Velociraptor				
Sense	Very Good	Good	Fair	Unable to Say
Sight	✔			
Hearing	✔			
Smell	✔			
Taste				✔
Touch				✔

Velociraptor Fossils

Velociraptor fossils have been found in China, Mongolia, and Russia.

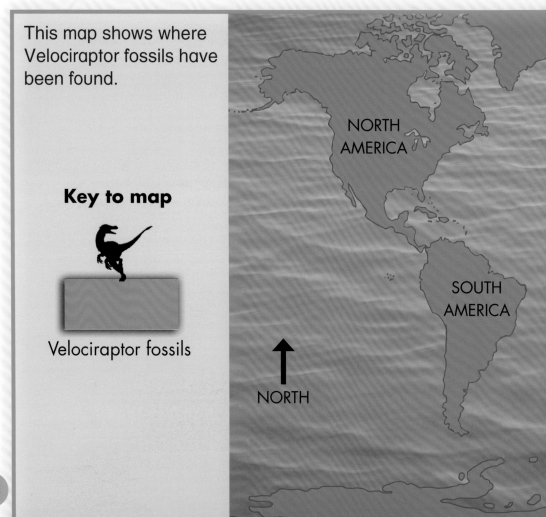

This map shows where Velociraptor fossils have been found.

Key to map

Velociraptor fossils

NORTH AMERICA

SOUTH AMERICA

NORTH

In 1922, paleontologists from the American Museum of Natural History found the first Velociraptor fossils. They found a skull and a claw in the Gobi Desert, in Mongolia.

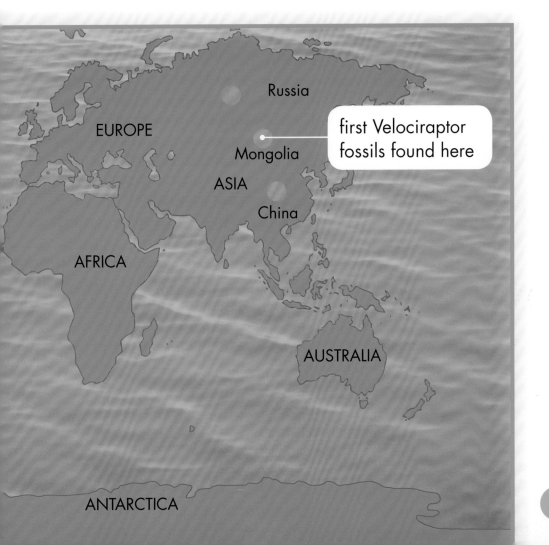

Russia

EUROPE

first Velociraptor
fossils found here

Mongolia

ASIA

China

AFRICA

AUSTRALIA

ANTARCTICA

Where Did Velociraptor Live?

Velociraptor lived in deserts with large hills of sand. These hills, called dunes, were formed by the wind. The deserts also had some streams and lakes.

Velociraptor had to find shade so it could survive in its desert home.

dunes

The deserts where Velociraptor lived had a hot and dry **climate**, just like most deserts today. Only tough plants, such as cycads and palms, could grow.

palms

cycads

What Did Velociraptor Eat?

Velociraptor was a carnivore, or meat-eater. It ate plant-eating dinosaurs, such as Protoceratops (*pro-toh-ser-ah-tops*). It probably also ate small **mammals** and lizards.

Foods Eaten by Velociraptor	
Protoceratops	
Small mammals	
Lizards	

Paleontologists think Velociraptor was a hunter.
They think it caught and ate small animals that also
lived in the desert.

Velociraptor probably watched its prey carefully and would
sneak up on it before attacking it.

Predator or Prey?

Velociraptor was a small and deadly **predator**. It probably ran very quickly and leapt at its prey. It then gripped its prey with its powerful claws and sharp teeth.

Velociraptor could leap high into the air because it had a light, powerful body.

Velociraptor had a huge claw on the second toe of each foot. It held these claws up when walking. It flicked them downward to pierce the skin of its prey.

Velociraptor used the huge claw on each foot to hold onto its prey.

How Did Velociraptor Live?

Dinosaurs similar to Velociraptor lived and hunted in packs. However, some paleontologists think Velociraptor lived alone. This is because there is no proof that it lived in packs.

Velociraptor may have lived alone.

Velociraptor spent its time resting and hunting for food. It probably hunted animals that stopped to drink at streams and lakes.

Velociraptor may have run as fast as 25 miles (40 kilometers) per hour when hunting.

Life Cycle of Velociraptor

Paleontologists study fossils and living animals to learn about the life cycle of Velociraptor.

1. An adult male Velociraptor displayed his feathers to attract a female. The male and female **mated**.

4. The baby Velociraptors stayed with their mothers until they were old enough to hunt. They grew into adults.

They believe there were four main stages in the life cycle of Velociraptor. This is what it may have been like.

2. The female laid eggs in a nest in the sand. She sat on the eggs to keep them warm.

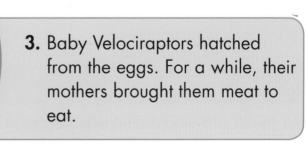

3. Baby Velociraptors hatched from the eggs. For a while, their mothers brought them meat to eat.

What Happened to Velociraptor?

Velociraptor became **extinct** about 65 million years ago. Many paleontologists think it died out when a large **meteorite** hit Earth. A meteorite would have caused most plants and animals to die.

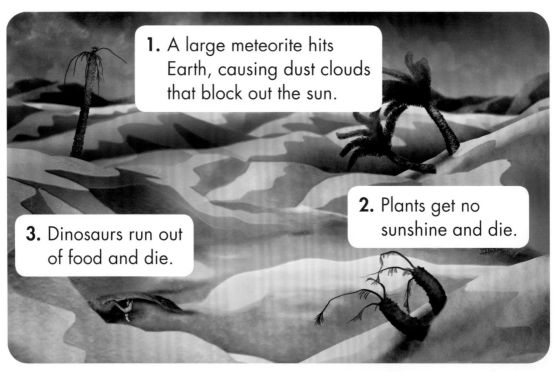

1. A large meteorite hits Earth, causing dust clouds that block out the sun.

2. Plants get no sunshine and die.

3. Dinosaurs run out of food and die.

A meteorite would also have caused earthquakes that shook the land and forced the dunes to collapse.

Some paleontologists think Velociraptor was dying out before the meteorite hit Earth. This is because Earth's climate was changing. Also, volcanoes were releasing **lava** and poisonous gases, which would have affected Velociraptor.

Velociraptor could not survive changing conditions on Earth, leaving us with only fossils.

Names and Their Meanings

Dinosaurs are named by people who discover them or paleontologists who study them. A dinosaur may be named for its appearance or behavior. Its name may also honor a person or place.

Name	Meaning
Dinosaur	Terrible lizard—because people thought dinosaurs were powerful lizards
Ankylosaurus	Fused lizard—because many of its bones were joined together
Diplodocus	Double beam—because it had special bones in its tail
Muttaburrasaurus	Muttaburra lizard—because it was discovered near the town of Muttaburra, in Australia
Protoceratops	First horned face—because it was one of the early horned dinosaurs
Tyrannosaurus	Tyrant lizard—because it was a fearsome ruler of the land
Velociraptor	Speedy thief—because it ran quickly and ate meat

Glossary

climate The usual weather in a place.

extinct No longer existing.

lava The very hot, melted rock that flows out of a volcano.

mammals Animals that feed their young with their own milk.

mated Created offspring.

meteorite A rock from space that has landed on Earth.

predator An animal that hunts and kills other animals for food.

prey An animal that is hunted and killed by other animals for food.

reptiles Creeping or crawling animals that are covered with scales.

senses A special ability that people and animals use to experience the world around them. Typically, those senses are sight, hearing, smell, taste, and touch.

skeletons The bones inside the body of a person or an animal.

Index

B

bird-hipped dinosaurs, 6, 7
brain, 14

C

carnivores, 20
claws, 8, 13, 17, 22, 23
Cretaceous period, 5, 11

D

deserts, 17, 18, 19, 21

E

eggs, 8, 27
extinction, 28, 29

F

feathers, 13, 26
food, 7, 20, 25, 28
fossils, 8, 9, 16–17, 26, 29

J

Jurassic period, 5, 11

L

life cycle, 26–27
lizard-hipped dinosaurs, 6, 7, 10

M

meat-eating dinosaurs, 7, 10, 20, 27, 30
Mesozoic Era, 5, 11

p

paleontologists, 9, 17, 21, 24, 26, 28, 29, 30
plant-eating dinosaurs, 7, 20
predators, 22
prey, 15, 21, 22, 23

R

reptiles, 4

S

senses, 15
skeletons, 9
skin, 23
skulls, 7, 14, 17

T

tail, 13, 30
teeth, 8, 14, 22
Triassic period, 5, 11